ludovico einaudi

[extra elements]

CHESTER MUSIC
part of The Wise Music Group

GREENPEACE

Published by
CHESTER MUSIC LIMITED
14-15 Berners Street, London W1T 3LJ, UK.

Exclusive Distributors:
HAL LEONARD
7777 West Bluemound Road,
Milwaukee, WI 53213
Email: info@halleonard.com

HAL LEONARD EUROPE LIMITED
42 Wigmore Street, Marylebone,
London WIU 2 RY
Email: info@halleonardeurope.com

HAL LEONARD AUSTRALIA PTY. LTD.
4 Lentara Court, Cheltenham,
Victoria 9132, Australia
Email: info@halleonard.com.au

Order No. CH85525
ISBN: 978-1-78558-470-1
This book © Copyright 2016 Chester Music.

Arranged for solo piano by the composer.
Additional arrangements by Alistair Watson.
Edited by Sam Lung.
Sub-edited by Louise Unsworth.
Music engraved and processed by Sarah Lofthouse, SEL Music Art Ltd.
Illustrations by Ludovico Einaudi.

Original CD design by Cristiano Di Giovanni.
Pages 4 and 6 images courtesy of Greenpeace/Pedro Armestre.
Printed in the EU.

www.wisemusicclassical.com
www.halleonard.com

elegy for the arctic

drop solo

twice solo

elegy for the arctic
extended version

When I first wrote *Elements* I saw a seemingly chaotic mix of images, thoughts and feelings which came together into my world — a map, sometimes clear and distinct, sometimes overlapped. As I continued to play the music, often on my own at the piano, the elements began to vary and take a different shape.

This book contains the solo versions for Drop and Twice. These reflect the fact that a musical text is like a living being, constantly evolving and changing, and that with any idea there is an endless potential of transformation. With this idea in mind I also invite you to explore your own variations of *Elements*.

Further included are two versions of Elegy For The Arctic, which I composed to support the Greenpeace campaign 'Save The Arctic'. For this I wanted to express the idea of eternity and fragility that I had felt in that place. The glacier is so immensely powerful, yet on the brink of eradication. This fragility of life is something which we often forget; this is my musical reflection on the Arctic.

www.greenpeace.org
www.savethearctic.org

elegy for the arctic

Ludovico Einaudi

Additional content available at
www.ch84205.com

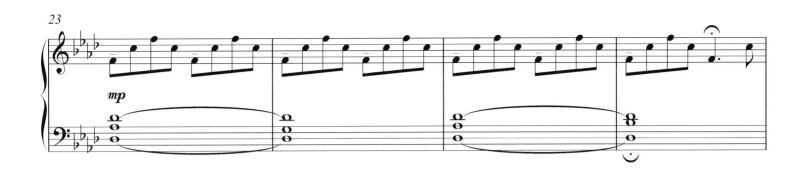

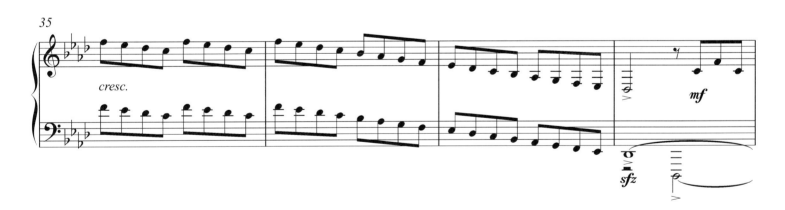

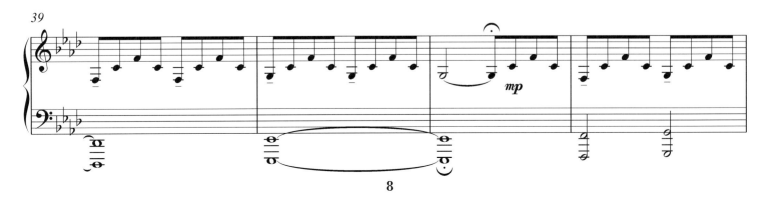

drop solo

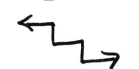

Ludovico Einaudi

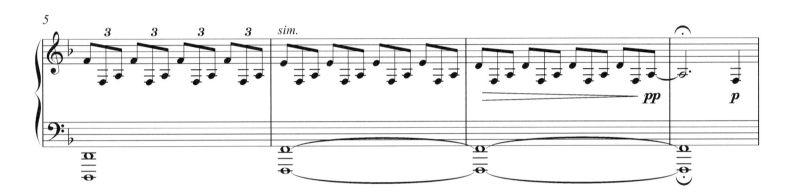

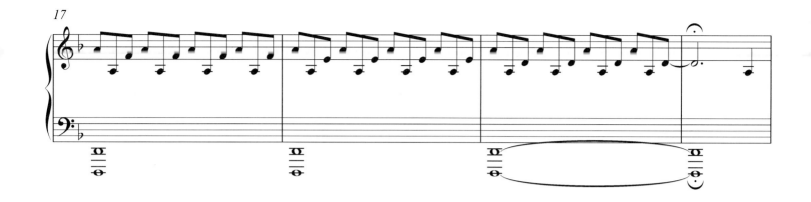

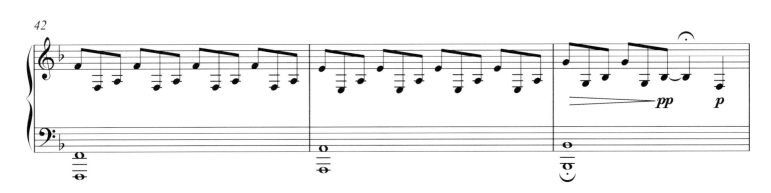

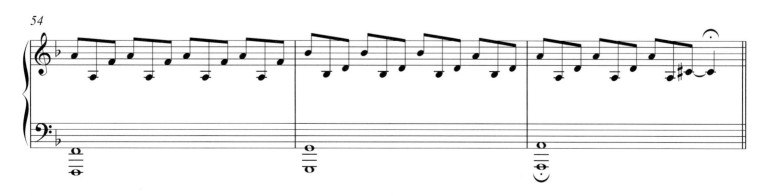

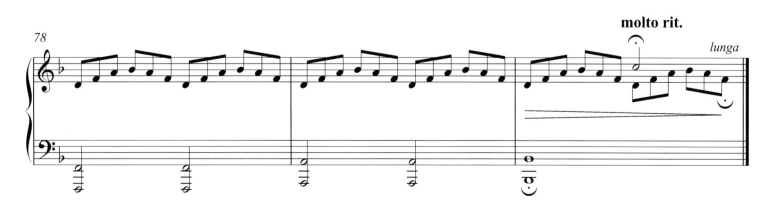

twice solo

Ludovico Einaudi

♩ = 120 Moderato

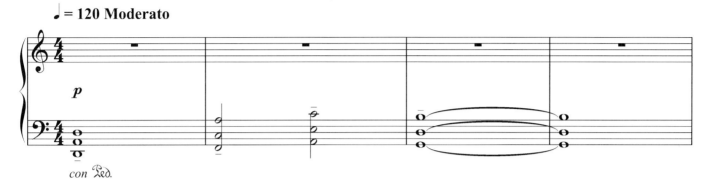

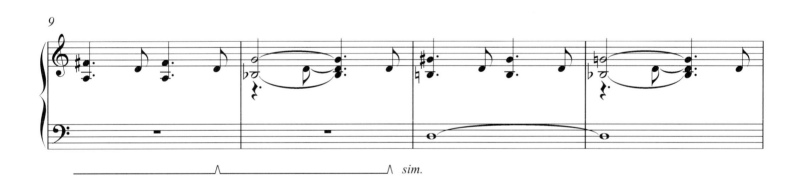

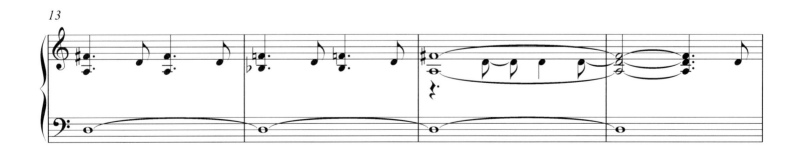

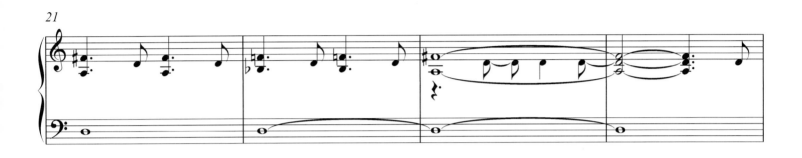

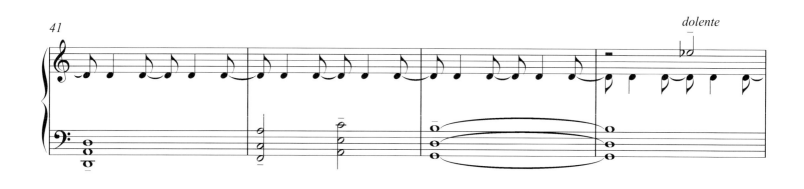

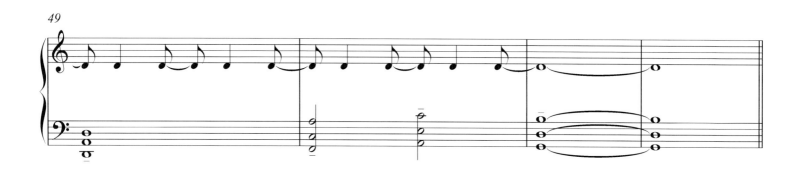

♩ = 100 **Meno mosso**

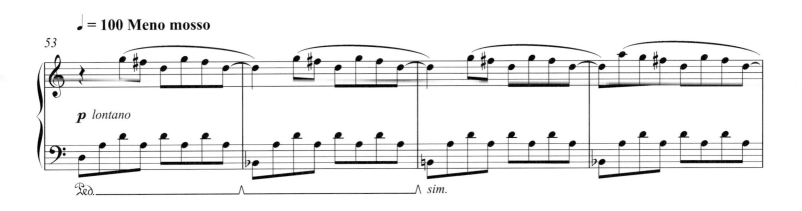

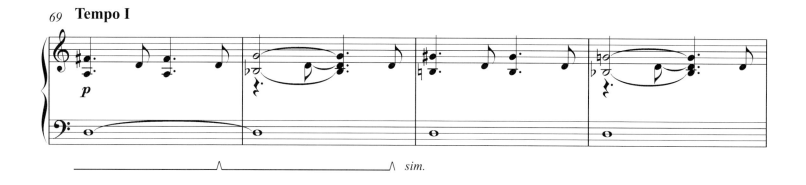

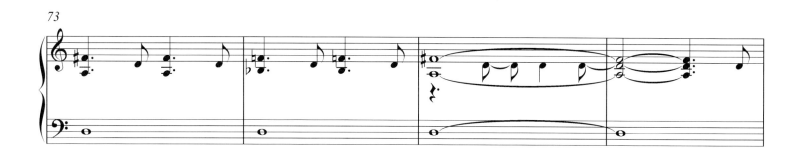

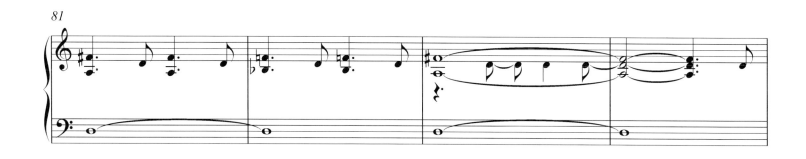

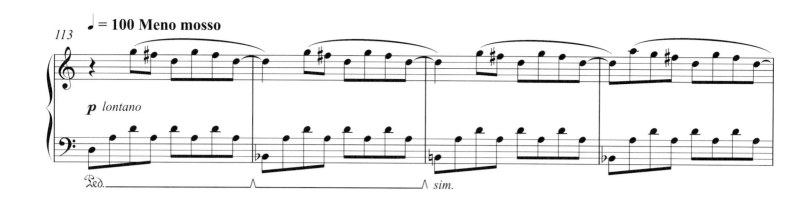

con Ped.

elegy for the arctic
extended version

Ludovico Einaudi

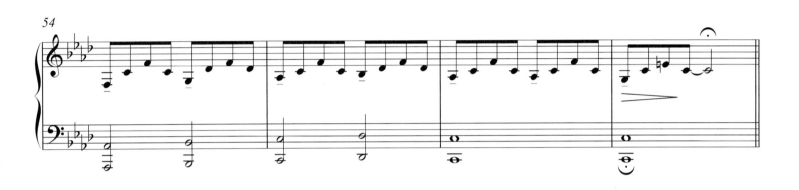

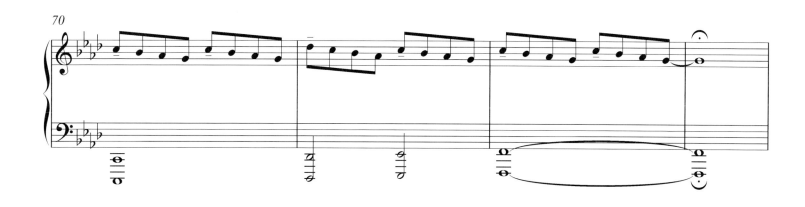

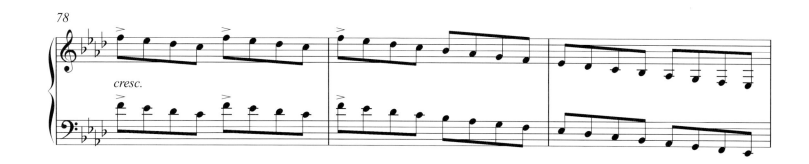

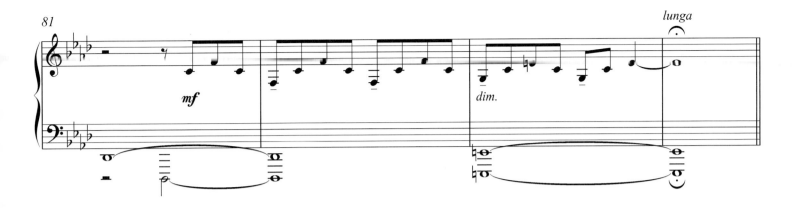

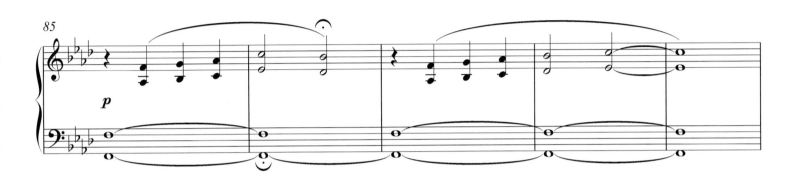

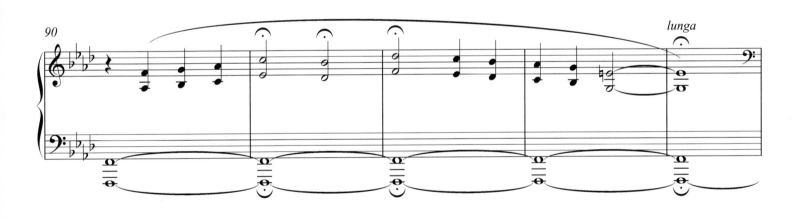

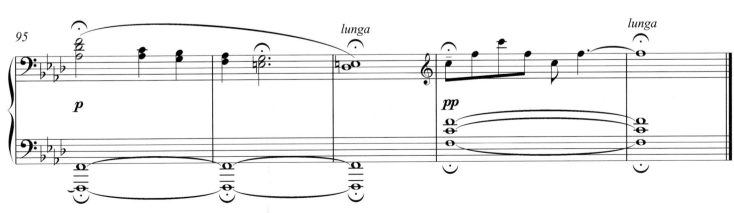

Una Mattina
AM91301

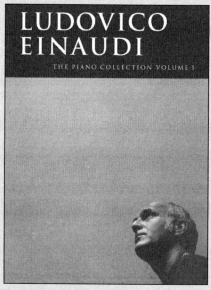

The Piano Collection Volume 1
AM91961

Divenire
CH72006

Islands
CH78518

Nightbook
CH76043

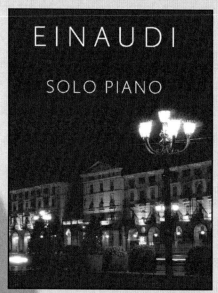

Solo Piano *(Slipcase Edition)*
CH80278

In A Time Lapse
AM80982

Film Music
CH83677

Elements
CH84205

LUDOVICO EINAUDI
Published by Chester Music
part of The Wise Music Group

These further Einaudi
piano volumes
are available from
all good music shops